PORTRAIT OF
COUNTY DOWN

SIMON BROWN

HALSGROVE

First published in Great Britain in 2009

Copyright © Simon Brown 2009

British Library Cataloguing-in-Publication Data
A CIP record for this title is available from the British Library

ISBN 978 1 84114 984 4

HALSGROVE
Halsgrove House,
Ryelands Industrial Estate,
Bagley Road, Wellington, Somerset TA21 9PZ
Tel: 01823 653777   Fax: 01823 216796
email: sales@halsgrove.com

Part of the Halsgrove group of companies.
Information on all Halsgrove titles is available at: www.halsgrove.com

Printed and bound by Grafiche Flaminia, Italy

Introduction

Most landscape photographers will be able to point fondly to a certain geographical area where they first honed their camera skills and fell in love with photography. For me it was my beloved home county of Down in Northern Ireland. County Down has been a wonderful photographic canvas for me over the past few years. It has everything I really need to satisfy my thirst for beautiful scenery to photograph. From enchanting harbours to majestic mountains to ancient ruins - it has so many visual pleasures to offer the admiring viewer.

County Down (derived from the Irish Contae an Dúin, meaning "County of the Fort") is one of the nine counties that form the province of Ulster and one of six counties that form Northern Ireland. Bordering County Antrim to the north, the Irish Sea to the east and County Armagh to the west, the county forms an area of 2,448 km2 (945 square miles). For such a relatively small area of land, however, County Down is positively saturated with areas of interest for the fortunate visitor to savour. And, unlike many other frequently lauded parts of the world, there is no need to endure endless days of road travel to take in the sights. No matter where you are in the county you will always be no more than a short drive away from somewhere that will take your breath away.

Despite having spent roughly the past seven years travelling around County Down with my camera, I still cannot claim to have witnessed all the beauty it has to offer. In truth, rarely a month goes by that I do not stumble across a picturesque part of the coastline, a thought-provoking site of historical significance or a luscious landscape that is new to my eyes. I am constantly learning more about and getting further acquainted with the lands where I have lived for most of my life. I know it will be a never-ending quest. The ever-changing and often unpredictable weather in this part of the world means that each scene looks very different every time I return to it.

This book is my own photographic tribute to these lands. In it I will endeavour to show you the well-known landmarks and landscapes of County Down at their most alluring. These are the sights that you will undoubtedly have seen in the local tourism guidebooks or that you may even have been lucky enough to be a spectator to yourself. But, as well as these, I will also strive to show you many of the hidden gems that you may not have seen. Those views that are only accessible by veering off the recommended walking trails or that only really come alive at certain times of the day, when the rising or setting sun casts its heavenly light over the land. In essence, this book is a visual depiction of my journey as I attempt to build a collection of images that do justice to the wonderfully refined lands of County Down.

Our journey begins in North Down, just a short distance away from Northern Ireland's largest city of Belfast. The attractive North Down Coastal Path follows the southern shores of Belfast Lough from Holywood to Bangor, taking in the scenic views from Helen's Bay and Crawfordsburn Country Park along the way. The seaside town of Bangor has historically been one of Northern Ireland's main tourist destinations, primarily acting as a haven for residents of Belfast keen to escape city life for a few days. In recent years, however, visitors have been attracted from further afield as a result of the seafront regeneration of the 1980s and '90s. This regeneration saw the construction of Ireland's second largest marina within the town's harbour that is now used as the setting for a variety of major sailing and tourist events each year.

Continuing along the coastline to the east of Bangor you begin the journey along the picturesque Ards Peninsula. The peninsula is an extremely photogenic finger of land that separates Strangford Lough from the North Channel of the Irish Sea. The two roads that run the length of the Peninsula on opposite sides offer very different photographic opportunities. The eastern side is littered with sandy beaches and charming harbours while the western side gives great views of Strangford Lough itself.

Among the most captivating sights on the eastern side of the peninsula is the lighthouse that dominates the scene at Donaghadee harbour. The lighthouse was built in the early nineteenth century and still gives sailors a safe passage in to the harbour to this day. A little further south is located the only remaining working windmill in County Down. The Ballycopeland Windmill in Millisle was built in the eighteenth century and, after lying unused for many decades, was restored to full working order in 1978. On the western side of the peninsula one of the highlights is the splendid ruins of a twelfth century Cistercian abbey in Greyabbey. The abbey is set in the beautifully landscaped gardens and parkland of Rosemount House and was the first Gothic building in Ireland.

At the southern end of the Ards Peninsula, the town of Portaferry lies at the entrance to Strangford Lough. This entrance is known as the Narrows and for a very good reason. The opening from Portaferry across the Narrows to Strangford village is just 0.5km wide, resulting in very strong currents when the waters rush in from the Irish Sea at high tide. The lough itself is the largest inlet in the British Isles, covering some 150km. According to legend there are 365 islands in Strangford Lough, one for every day of the year. These islands are most prevalent on the western shore of the lough which is fringed by a multitude of partly submerged hills known as drumlins which were formed by glacial action during the last Ice Age.

A short ferry ride across the turbulent waters of the Narrows will take you to the low-lying Lecale Peninsula. Up until about 200 years ago the Lecale Peninsula was fairly isolated from the bordering area, surrounded by Strangford Lough to the north, the Irish Sea to the east and south and by the Quoile marshland to the west. The marshland area is now drained and in 1957 the construction of a tidal barrier across the estuary of the river helped to create the wildlife rich Quoile Pondage National Nature Reserve.

All around the Lecale Peninsula and its closest neighbouring town of Downpatrick you will come across many references and relics celebrating the life of the patron saint of Ireland – Saint Patrick. Saint Patrick was kidnapped and taken to Ireland as a slave when he was about sixteen years of age. He eventually escaped after six years and returned to his family in Britain. After subsequently entering the church, Patrick later returned to Ireland as a missionary and, according to tradition, is said to have played a major part in converting the country of his previous captivity to Christianity. One of the most impressive reminders of Saint Patrick's legacy in the area is the 10 metre high statue on the summit of Slieve Patrick near the village of Saul.

The whole area around Downpatrick is steeped in history of various ages and one fascinating example of this is the Ballynoe Stone Circle. Over 50 large upright stones surround a space about 110 feet across with a 5 foot high mound of earth at its centre. The mound was excavated in the 1930s and stone cists containing cremated bones were found suggesting that the site was used as an ancient burial ground in the late Neolithic to earlier Bronze Age era. The existence of this and the many other megalithic structures found in County Down help give a tantalising insight into life in the area thousands of years ago.

As you move further south down the Lecale Peninsula the Mourne Mountains become an increasingly dominant part of the landscape. Amazing views of Northern Ireland's largest mountain range can be had from St John's Point near Killough and from the beach at Tyrella. But perhaps the most memorable view of the Mournes is the vista seen from the beach at the Murlough Nature Reserve. This 5 mile stretch of golden sand is the perfect place to stand and watch the sun setting over the peak of Slieve Donard. Murlough itself is a fragile 6,000 year old sand dune system which became Northern Ireland's first nature reserve in 1967. A network of paths and boardwalks wind their way through the heath-covered dunes down to the beach. Many a gasp of admiration has been heard over the years as visitors step out on to the beach for the first time to witness the iconic view.

For all the joys that viewing the Mournes from a distance brings, there really is nothing like seeing them close up. The Mourne Mountains truly are the visual gem of County Down. These rugged, granite peaks (14 of which are over 600 metres high) provide a rejuvenating wilderness landscape for the thousands of people who walk amongst them every year. Standing on top of Slieve Donard, at 849 metres the highest mountain in Northern Ireland, you can easily forget that the hustle and bustle of daily modern life is still taking place on the streets below you. It is obvious why the whole mountain region has been designated an Area of Outstanding Beauty. Although undoubtedly the main appeal of the mountains is their untouched and natural essence, there is one man-made feature that seems to only add to their beauty. The spectacular Mourne Wall sprawls for 35 impressive kilometres across 15 of the surrounding peaks and, rather than spoil the views, serves only to add to the awe-inducing sense of scale you feel whilst walking amongst the mountains. Standing 2 metres high and a metre thick, the wall was built between 1904 and 1922 to provide work during a period of high unemployment and to enclose the catchment area of the Silent Valley and the Annalong River.

Lying at the heart of the Mourne Mountains, the Silent Valley Reservoir provides a peaceful haven for those who don't feel quite able to tackle the strenuous mountain slopes. Scenic pathways lead you on quiet walks around the grounds whilst a 4 kilometre jaunt up the side of the reservoir will take you to the Ben Crom Dam. The Silent Valley Reservoir, along with the nearby Ben Crom Reservoir, supplies 30 million gallons of water a day to Belfast and County Down and was considered to be one of the greatest engineering achievements ever when it was opened in 1933. Most visitors to the area, however, are too spellbound by the reservoir's beauty to appreciate the expertise involved in its creation.

No photographic book about County Down would be complete without at least an admiring reference to the wondrous woodlands it contains within its boundaries. Two of the most striking examples are the Tollymore and Castlewellan forest parks, both of which can be found just north of the Mournes. Covering an area of almost 500 hectares, Tollymore Forest Park provides spectacular views of the surrounding mountains. The Shimna River flows through the centre of the park, winding its way merrily to meet the sea at Newcastle. The river also helps act as a guide to the many walkers who enjoy following its path through the park's scenic woodland. At 450 hectares Castlewellan Forest Park is only slightly smaller in size to Tollymore, but is no less impressive. A forest of conifer and broadleaf woodland surrounds the splendid Castlewellan Lake whose circumference kindly affords visitors with a gentle and accessible tree-lined walking route. As the name suggests, the grounds in the forest park are also home to a castle. This Scottish baronial castle, which dates back to 1856, is situated in an idyllic location overlooking the lake and forest.

And so we come to the end of our journey around County Down. Along the way we have savoured the scenic coastline of North Down and taken in the captivating sights of the Ards Peninsula. We have steeped ourselves in the history of the Lecale Peninsula and taken leisurely walks through the picturesque forests at Tollymore and Castlewellan. And, of course, we have been admiring viewers of the majestic Mourne Mountains both from afar and from within their rugged peaks. I can't claim to have shown you everything the county has to offer. There are, I'm sure, many more pleasures that it has yet to show me and which I shall strive to capture in the future. But hopefully you have enjoyed the places that we have been to. As I said in the beginning, I consider myself to be extremely fortunate to live in County Down. As a photographer it provides me with endless opportunities to indulge in my love for taking pictures. The photographs included in this book are all the result of a passionate quest to capture my beloved County Down at its finest. When I look at each picture I can still remember how I felt when I took it. The awe, the fascination, the joy at being witness to such a memorable scene. I hope you enjoy viewing these scenes as much as I enjoyed capturing them with my camera.

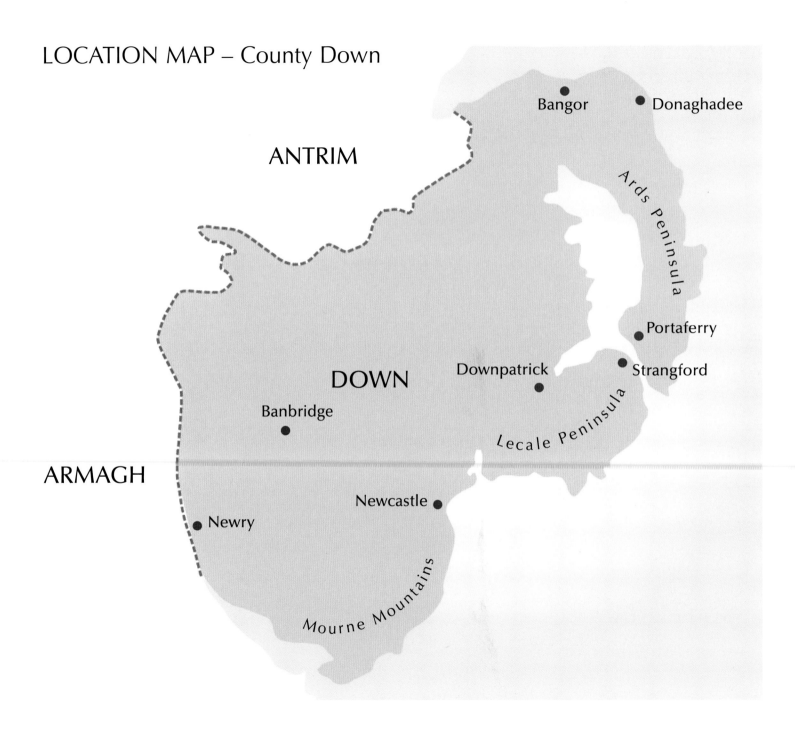

LOCATION MAP – County Down

Bangor

Donaghadee

ANTRIM

Ards Peninsula

Portaferry

DOWN

Downpatrick

Strangford

Banbridge

Lecale Peninsula

ARMAGH

Newcastle

Newry

Mourne Mountains

Looking towards the Belfast Hills from the Kinnegar jetty in Holywood

Sunset over the Holywood shoreline

The jetty and slipway at Holywood Yacht Club

A forest scene in Cairn Wood

Light and shadows in Cairn Wood

A farming scene in County Down

A boat house at Helen's Bay on the North Down coast

The Crawfordsburn coastline

Right:
A waterfall in Crawfordsburn
Country Park

Sunset over the North Down coastal path

Left:
The North Down coastal path

An abandoned boat house on the North Down coast

Sunset over Wilsons Point on the North Down coast

The Eisenhower Pier on Bangor seafront

A sunset viewed from behind the Eisenhower Pier in Bangor

Bregenz House and Bangor Marina

The promenade at Bangor Marina

Boats moored in Bangor Marina

A sunset scene on the Long Hole Pier in Bangor

Sailing at sunset in Ballyholme on the outskirts of Bangor

Right:
Moonlight on Ballyholme Beach

Dusk on Ballyholme Beach

A heart drawn in the sand on Ballyholme Beach

The view from Ballyholme promenade

A twilight scene on calm waters at Ballyholme

Groomsport Harbour

Groomsport Harbour at dusk

Steps to the sunset in Groomsport

Left:
Sunset over Groomsport Harbour

The lighthouse
and harbour in
Donaghadee

Right:
Twilight
reflections of the
Donaghadee
Lighthouse

Lighthouse and buoy at Donaghadee Harbour

Reflections along Donaghadee seafront

The Moat Castle in Donaghadee

The sun's rays splitting the clouds on Millisle Beach

Ballycopeland Windmill in Millisle

Ballycopeland Windmill at sunset

Inside an old blacksmith's workshop in Millisle

Dawn breaks over an outdoor swimming pool in Millisle

A standing stone
monument in
Millisle

Right:
Low tide at
Ballywalter
Harbour

The "Echoes of Awareness 2001" sculpture in Ballywalter

Right:
Hay bales at dawn in Portaferry

A wintry dawn on Windmill Hill in Portaferry

Lough Cowey near
Portaferry

Lough Cowey at
dusk

The Millin Bay Cairn at sunset

The Saint Cooeys Wells located near Portaferry at the southern tip of the Ards Peninsula

Kircubbin Harbour

The graveyard and ruins at Greyabbey

The shores of Strangford Lough at Greyabbey

The house and gardens at Mount Stewart

Right:
Lakeside at Mount Stewart

The Temple of the Winds at Mount Stewart

Sunset on the western side of the Ards Peninsula

Reflections at low tide on Strangford Lough

Rays of sunshine over Strangford Lough

Tracks disappearing into the twilight on Strangford Lough

Sea simplicity on Strangford Lough

Halcyon horizon on the Ards Peninsula

Fiery farewell over the Ards Peninsula

The pier and clubhouse at Newtownards Sailing Club

The pier and slipway at Newtownards Sailing Club

Rocks disappearing into the sunset on the Ards Peninsula

The shores of Strangford Lough at sunset

A distant view of Scrabo Tower at sunset

Scrabo Tower viewed at low tide from the shores of Strangford Lough

Scrabo Tower silhouetted against a fiery sunset sky

The path to
Scrabo Tower

Right:
Scrabo Tower at
dawn

Islandhill Nature Reserve

Moonlight over the Islandhill
Nature Reserve

Boats moored in Whiterock Bay

Twilight mirrored on the waters at Mahee Island

Nendrum Monastic Site

Nendrum Monastic Site at dusk

Calm waters of Strangford Lough at Killinchy

Right:
Ballymorran Bay near Killinchy

Ballymorran Bay at dusk

Strangford Lough drumlins

Farmland around Strangford Lough

Audley's Castle near Strangford

Castle Ward boathouse

Bluebells in Delamont Country Park

The Strangford Stone in Delamont Country Park

The Quoile River

A jetty on the edge of the Quoile River

A statue of Saint Patrick at the top of Slieve Patrick

A crucifixion scene on Slieve Patrick

Saul Church

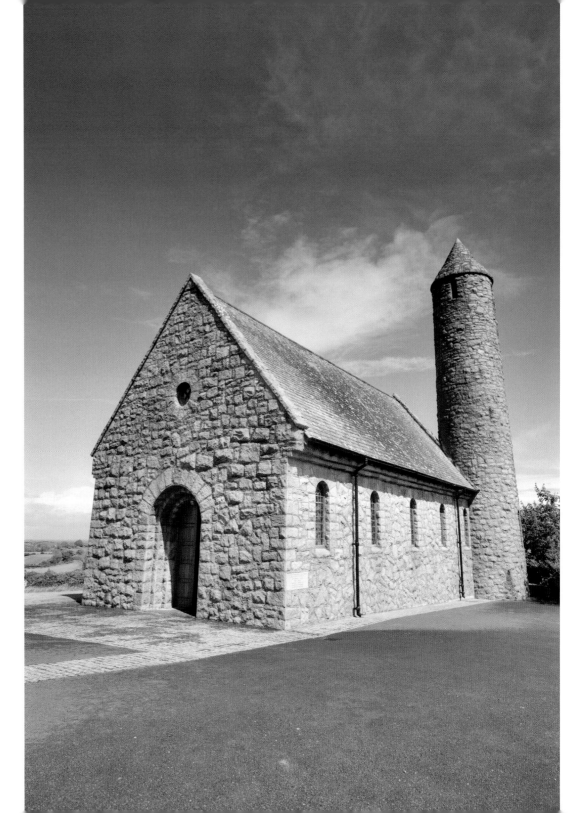

The sun's rays split the clouds below Slieve Patrick

Inch Abbey

Struell Wells

Ballynoe Stone Circle

Clough Castle

Legananny Dolmen

St John's Point
Lighthouse

Right:
Dusk at St John's
Point

Sunrise over Dundrum

Dundrum Castle

Loughmoney Dolmen

Greencastle

Haulbowline Lighthouse as seen from
Cranfield Point

The Cloughmore Stone in Kilbroney
Forest Park

A waterfall in Kilbroney Forest Park

Reeds blowing in the wind on the County Down coast

Right:
A stormy sunset on the County Down coast

Waves breaking on the shore on the County Down coast

A sunset scene along the
County Down coast

A path through Hillsborough Forest Park

The lake in Hillsborough Forest Park

Slieve Croob

Looking down the Transmitter Road on Slieve Croob

Sunset on Tyrella Beach

The Slidderyford Bridge near Newcastle

A broken fence in
Murlough Nature
Reserve

Murlough Beach

Sunset on Murlough Beach at low tide

The Mourne Mountains as seen from St John's Point

The Mourne Mountains reflecting on Tyrella Beach

A view of the Mournes at low tide on Tyrella Beach

The Mourne Mountains as seen from the dunes at the Murlough National Nature Reserve

A sunset view of the Mourne Mountains from Murlough

The Wateresk Dolmen against the backdrop of the Mourne Mountains

A rainbow in the Mourne Mountains

The Silent Valley Reservoir

The mountains surrounding the Silent Valley
Reservoir

Spelga Dam

Spelga Dam viewed from the summit of Pigeon Rock Mountain

The summit of Butter Mountain in the Mournes

The Mourne Wall leading up Slieve Commedagh

Right:
The Mourne Wall at the top of Slieve Donard

The Hares Gap

Left:
Low cloud over the Mourne Wall at Hares Gap

Windy Gap viewed from the summit of Eagle Mountain

The Blue Lough situated amongst the Mourne Mountains

The Ben Crom Reservoir

Left:
The Ben Crom Dam

A hillside cottage in
the Mournes

The Mourne Mountains
as seen from the
Carrick Little track

Trees casting long shadows over frosty fields near Newcastle

Sunrise on Newcastle Beach

Castlewellan Forest Park

Stepping Stones in Tollymore Forest Park